Durham Revisited

Then & Now

Contents

Dr C.W. Gibby   *Daisy Edis*

Acknowledgements

*T*his book has been compiled by members of Durham Photographic Society. We particularly wish to thank the following for material and information: Beamish North of England Open-Air Museum photographic library; University of Durham Library, Palace Green; Durham Clayport Library; Durham County Record Office; St Hild and St Bede College and the University Hospital of North Durham.

Members of Durham Photographic Society who made major contributions include Colin Armitstead, John Attle, Don Bennett, Jim Bennett, John Brown, Roger Culpin, Ken Durose, Alex Ellwood, Joe Grabham, Harry Holder, Maurice Sanderson, Alan Stott, Bill Swinburn, Janet Thackray, Malcolm Thurman, David Trout, John Tyrrell, Robin Wallace, David Wardle and Brian Wilcockson.

The University of Durham Library at Palace Green holds the original copies of the old photographs shown on pages 9, 11, 15, 17, 19, 22, 23, 26, 30, 32, 33, 35, 36, 37, 38, 40, 41, 42, 43, 44, 45, 46, 47, 50, 51, 52, 55, 57, 58, 59, 65, 67, 68, 69, 70, 73, 75, 79, 83, 87, 90, 91, 92 and 93.

Introduction

The ever-changing face of Durham, one of England's most important historical cities, is a constant source of fascination for residents and visitors alike. For almost 1,000 years the skyline has been dominated by the world-famous cathedral and castle towering on a rock above the River Wear, while down in the city centre beautiful Georgian and Victorian façades give an impression of permanence. But change is constant. Just look at photographs taken just ten to twenty years ago, never mind those dating back fifty to a hundred years, and the rate of progress can only be described as amazing. If only we had photographs from centuries ago, what insights they would have given us into the Durham of medieval times or when Tudor monarchs ruled. As it is, our local photographic heritage reaches back in time rather less than 150 years.

The history of Durham dates back more than 1,000 years. It was in AD 995 that the city was to become the shrine of St Cuthbert. He had died around 300 years earlier but his coffin was removed from its resting place on Lindisfarne due to the threat of Viking invasions on the Northumbrian coast. Monks guarding his remains toured the region for centuries, with rests at Chester-le-Street and Ripon, until finally settling at Durham. Here they built a Saxon church to contain his shrine, it being completed in 1017. After the Norman Conquest, King William selected Durham as the centre of his administration in Northern England. Work began on the castle in 1072 and the mighty new Norman cathedral – on which work began in 1093 – replaced the comparatively recent Saxon church. This new cathedral also became the shrine to St Bede, whose tomb, like that of St Cuthbert, is housed there. The city grew up round the castle and cathedral, with medieval houses nestling in their shadow for centuries. Over time, bridges were built across the River Wear and a network of highways gradually developed.

Huge alterations have taken place in the short space of time since 1999 when Durham Photographic Society last compiled a Then & Now book on the city to mark the new millennium. Roads have been altered to improve traffic flows, particularly in the North Road and Millburngate areas, Victorian-style town houses have been erected, and the new £100 million University Hospital of North Durham, built to replace the old Dryburn Hospital, has been constructed. So this seems an appropriate time to revisit the archives and revive old material for decades hidden from public gaze. As in the last volume, members of Durham Photographic Society have selected old pictures and have then photographed the same scenes from a modern-day perspective. Many of these old pictures came from the records at Beamish Museum and others from Durham University's collection of work by the late Dr C.W. Gibby and the noted photographic business of John Edis and his daughter Daisy Edis. Appropriately for the Photographic Society, Daisy Edis was once a member and her name is perpetuated on one of the Society's competition trophies. Her father, John Reed Edis (1860-1942), was one of the first students to enrol as a photographer at Quintin Hogg's newly founded polytechnic in London.

He established a business in Durham in the 1890s and became official photographer to the Dean and Chapter, Durham University and to Durham School. He also gained a reputation as a landscape photographer. When he died in 1942, the business was continued by his daughter Daisy, who had worked with him since 1901. She ran the business from a shop in Saddler Street until 1964. Daisy, who became a portrait specialist, married George Spence but always maintained her maiden name. Long-time member of Durham Photographic Society Harry Holder remembers her as a formidable lady at the camera club. Fellow members of the society always addressed her as Miss Edis, never by her Christian name.

Dr Clifton William Gibby (1902-1989), a noted local historian, was widely known as Jack. He lived in the city's fine South Street, which overlooks the cathedral and castle. From 1929 he was a lecturer in chemistry at the university and in 1968 became an honorary research associate in the Archaeology Department. He was a popular and stimulating lecturer both in his university department and also when he gave talks on the history of Durham. Dr Gibby's fascination with local history led him to take and acquire a large collection of photographs of the city. He later donated this collection to the university. Thanks to early photographers and collectors like John and Daisy Edis and Dr Gibby, we have a rich treasure of Durham scenes from earlier generations.

In the City of Durham, changes have met with various degrees of controversy, some people maintaining that all change is for the worse. But change can be for the better. Imagine the horror of Durham's pre-1960s road system attempting to cope with modern traffic conditions. The narrow streets in the city centre, now largely traffic-free, have become pedestrian-friendly areas thanks to a modern network of roads and bridges which bypass the centre. Many of the old houses torn down in the early twentieth century, whatever their historic interest, were little better than slums. Now the 1930s council houses built at Sherburn Road to replace these old slums have recently themselves been extensively modernised to bring them up to twenty-first-century standards. The replacement of the run-down Dryburn Hospital with the private sector-funded University Hospital of North Durham attracted political criticism. Yet few could argue against the benefits of the modern building, which is fitted with the latest in medical technology.

These continuing changes, for better and for worse, have been recorded by generations of photographers of the nineteenth, twentieth and twenty-first centuries, including by members of Durham Photographic Society. The Society itself has seen big changes. The first camera club in Durham was launched in 1892 and met in the Shakespeare Hall in North Road. Defunct after the First World War, this club was succeeded briefly by other similar organisations between the wars. In the late 1940s the present Durham Photographic Society was launched and met in a variety of venues until moving back to the Shakespeare Hall in North Road in the late 1970s. In 2004 the club moved yet again, this time to St Oswald's Church Institute.

In *Durham Revisited*, whether it is in buildings, roads, fashion or the nature of an event like the Miners' Gala, the changes are there for all to see.

Please note that throughout the book the larger photograph of each pair is the older one.

North Road

An atmospheric night-time picture of a deserted North Road taken in 1936. The entrance to what was the Regal cinema is seen on the left.

*D*urham's most important development of the early twenty-first century has been the opening of the University Hospital of North Durham. This £100 million hi-tech health facility for the twenty-first century is one of Britain's pioneering Private Finance Initiative hospitals, jointly built by the NHS and private enterprise. The buildings are owned and maintained by the private sector but healthcare is still controlled and administered by the NHS. Work started on the complex in April 1998 and the first patients moved in during April 2001.

The new hospital, catering for the population of a much wider area in the north of the county, replaces the old Dryburn Hospital, much of which was housed in run-down wooden-built wards dating back several generations. The large old-fashioned wards have gone and in their place are smaller and more intimate rooms. State-of-the-art operating theatres have been built, fitted with the latest medical technology.

The hospital stands alongside North Road on the outskirts of Durham city centre. Down the hill, nearer the city centre, North Road is a busy shopping street. Nestling under the 1850s railway viaduct carrying the East Coast main line stands a small and attractive complex of nineteenth-century stone-built shops, plus the Bridge Inn. The corner shop is now occupied by Applejacks, a popular sandwich bar, but a variety of businesses have occupied the premises over the years. In the older photograph from the mid-twentieth century it was the premises of A. Watts, confectioner and tobacconist.

*T*his is the scene on North Road outside the bus station. What a colourful view this must have been back in the early 1900s when our earlier picture was taken.

Horse-drawn traffic, boys on bikes, girls in long frocks and stylish hats, and those striped and highly coloured shop awnings. The tower above the horse cart is that of the Miners' Hall, replaced as the official headquarters of the Durham Miners' Union in 1915 when a new building was opened at Redhills. Since then, the block has housed a variety of enterprises, including a cinema and a nightclub. The former Miners' Hall remains virtually unchanged, but the functional modern buildings on the site lack the charm of their earlier Victorian predecessors.

North Road and Miners Hall, Durham

*T*owards the top of North Road is Durham's busy bus station. From the early days of bus travel until the 1970s the bus lanes opened straight onto North Road from under an attractive iron and glass canopy. Our earliest picture was taken in 1934 by the one-time Northern General Transport Company to celebrate its twenty-one years of service to the population of the North East. Northern inaugurated one of the region's first scheduled services, from Chester-le-Street to Newcastle, in 1913. Rebuilt in the late twentieth century, the new bus station is concealed from the street behind a row of modern shops. In the present-day photograph a double-decker owned by Northern's current operator, the Go-Ahead Group, emerges from the exit to the bus station.

*M*any of the shop buildings in North Road have remained largely unaltered for generations. In these two views of No. 71, J. Tuke & Son, music and radio dealers, have given way to a clothing company, Parkin's.

The earlier photograph is dated October 1938 and shows a tobacconist's shop to the left of Tuke's. Madame Gray, who sold children's clothes and millinery for many years, occupied the premises on the right. Now North Road Jewellers on the left and the Food Weighouse on the right operate from these two shops. Above the shops is the Shakespeare Hall. It was here in the 1890s that Durham's first camera club was formed. Durham City Camera Club was the forerunner of today's Durham Photographic Society, which for many years met in the Shakespeare Hall before moving to St Oswald's Church Institute in 2004.

*T*he lower half of North Road now has limited traffic access. Once part of the Great North Road, it is now largely for pedestrians only, although buses and delivery lorries still use the route. This early 1960s view, showing Smith's furniture and carpet shop and Harton's the cleaners, gives the impression of spaciousness although even then the road could become uncomfortably congested at busy times. These shops, which were situated at the end of the road as seen in today's picture, were demolished in the late 1960s when Millburngate was re-routed. Recently, this part of North Road has been narrowed to one lane, with one-way traffic only for buses during daytime hours. Wider pavements give pedestrians more freedom to do their shopping, just as they had in the more leisurely age of horses and carts.

*T*he bottom of North Road, at a point just before it enters Framwellgate Bridge, forms a junction with South Street and Crossgate. Back in 1926 Alexander's Corner, as it was then known, was home to M. Alexander's jewellery shop. Later the corner shop was part of Archibalds, Durham's well-known hardware and building materials merchants. After Archibald's vacated the building for premises outside the city centre, the site was cleared and totally rebuilt during 1997 and 1998. Although the new premises, now occupied by the Halifax Bank, looks to be the same, it is in fact a new building constructed in sympathetic style to correspond to the original.

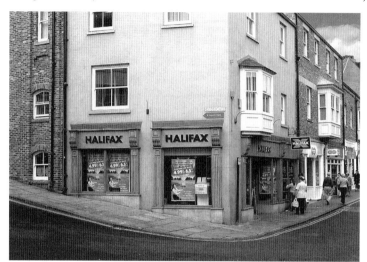

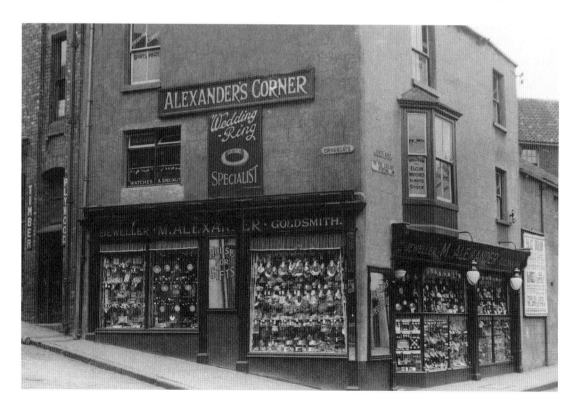

*I*n a picture that could never be repeated nowadays, a double-decker bus, bound for Bishop Auckland, trundles towards North Road from Framwellgate Bridge. The bus is emerging from a section of road which is vehicle-free today, but which was once one of the city's busiest in terms of traffic. The area seen in the picture was known as Five Ways, as it was the meeting point of North Road, Millburngate, South Street, Crossgate and Framwellgate Bridge and it gave its name to the pub on the extreme left, the Five Ways Inn. John Oliver's fishmongers shop is seen to the right of the inn at 131 Millburngate, a position it occupied for many years. Today, the original position of Millburngate can still be made out, as a gap between the buildings on this side of the shopping centre.

*A*n old and new view of the bottom end of South Street, one of Durham's most elegant thoroughfares, which begins in the commercial area near Framwellgate Bridge.

Alexander Gleason, tinsmith, occupied this shop at 3 South Street from before the Second World War into the 1950s. The little shop was sandwiched between two pubs, the Criterion and the Fighting Cocks. The new picture shows the Fighting Cocks is still there on the right, but all the buildings to the left of it have been rebuilt, including the tinsmith's which has been supplanted by Klick Photo Processing. Gleason's shop was removed to Beamish Museum, which features a number of shops set up to recreate life in the North East in days gone by. As yet it has still to be re-erected.

2

Framwellgate

Looking down Framwellgate as it was before
the demolitions of the 1930s.

This classic view of the cathedral and castle, taken around 1910, reveals a Framwellgate that is long gone. In the foreground, the jumble of houses and allotments gives a striking impression of the high density of population in this part of the city in former days. This was once a prosperous district, with merchants and tradesmen occupying the buildings on either side of the road, but after the seventeenth century it went into decline. By the mid-1800s the street was no longer the main route to the north after the construction of North Road and the once fine old houses became dilapidated to the point where they were slums. Many homes were swept away in the 1930s and by the 1970s there was no trace of this community. The modern picture shows how a new private housing development, Highgate, has changed the scene.

*A*nyone who has taken a trip to Durham by train cannot have failed to appreciate the marvellous elevated view of the city as they leave the railway station. The old picture was taken from this viewpoint in the 1980s and shows the grassy area that sloped down from the station to the old Framwellgate Road, off to the left. Before the 1930s this area was covered with allotments, but after the slum clearances of that time the Bishop of Durham took the opportunity to buy the land so that the view could be preserved. This remained the case until 1979, when Durham County Council obtained the area by Compulsory Purchase Order. The new picture shows how the recently built town houses of Highgate have, after all, radically altered the view.

The old photograph, from the 1960s, shows Castle Chare, a short terrace of a dozen houses situated across the road from St Godric's church. The milk had just been delivered as the photographer took this shot, looking down the hill to where the street joined the top of Millburngate. The spire of St Nicholas' church in the Market Place can be seen on the right. However, the fate of these homes had already been sealed when the picture was taken; the street was removed as part of the 1960 plan to reduce traffic congestion in the city centre. A new road, linking Millburngate Bridge to the top of North Road, would ease traffic flow in the latter, but it meant Castle Chare had to go. Today the roadway at Castle Chare is the same as in the original picture, but access to Millburngate is now blocked off. Pedestrians making for the railway station can make use of the footbridge which spans the new road, off to the left.

*I*n the 1950s, anyone travelling down
Framwellgate from the railway bridge
would have had this view to their left. The
Durham City Gas Works, a rather grim feature
of this area since the 1830s, can be seen on
the left-hand side, with the ice rink across the
river on the right. The short terrace of houses
aligned towards the centre of the ice rink is
Castle View. Fifty years later, the view could not

be more different. Millburngate House, which
now occupies practically the whole of this side
of Framwellgate, arrived to become the home
of National Savings in the late 1960s. The
employment this generated was welcomed,
but, while there were few tears over the
disappearance of the Gas Works, the design of
its successor left many Durham folk distinctly
unimpressed.

The simple mini roundabout shown in the old picture marked the bottom of Framwellgate in the 1970s. Beyond the roundabout, Framwellgate curves its way uphill to pass beneath a railway bridge, shrouded by trees on the horizon. Even at the time this picture was taken, it was difficult to imagine that, a hundred years before, this place supported over 1,000 people who occupied the 120 or so dwellings which lined both sides of the street. The inhabitants were typically labourers, miners, domestic servants and factory workers. By the time of the 1970s picture, no one actually lived along Framwellgate, although Millburngate House on the right and Lucas Auto Components on the left provided a population of sorts during working hours. The modern view shows how permanent residents have returned, at Highgate, top left. In the foreground, an ingenious new 'hamburger' roundabout has been installed to reduce traffic congestion here. The central channel provides a store for cars turning right into Millburngate and has reduced waiting times and tailbacks.

O ne of the last survivors of the old Framwellgate, Blagdon's Leather Works, stands in isolation shortly before its demolition. Durham was largely bypassed by the Industrial Revolution, but leather manufacture had a tradition in the city and the business that George Blagdon established here in 1854 was to remain a family concern for over a hundred years. The company provided a variety of leather goods for the home and foreign markets and received railway, colliery and government contracts. However, by the time it was demolished in March 1967, the works had become a rather depressing feature of an area made up of temporary car parks and waste ground. Four years later, the go-ahead was given for the construction of Millburngate Shopping Centre, shown in the new picture, the second phase of which has covered the Leather Works site since 1987.

As slum clearance in the Framwellgate area progressed from the late 1930s, there was a need to re-house the displaced residents. Many moved to the new estate on Sherburn Road, while others found accommodation in the council houses shown in the old photograph. These houses lined the western side of Millburngate below St Godric's Convent and School, seen in the background. There was some outrage when, in the 1960s, the realignment of the road necessitated the destruction of what were seen as perfectly sound buildings. In the recent picture, bus shelters now stand in place of the terrace. There is new housing in this area, but it has become decidedly up-market. The town houses of Highgate stand in the distance and the former school buildings of St Godric's have been converted into the bright modern apartments seen in the centre of the picture.

*F*ramwellgate Waterside in the early to mid-1960s. The end of the short terrace of houses called Lambton Walk, still occupied at the time, is seen on the left-hand side of the old picture. Within ten years it would be gone, along with most of the other structures seen in this view. The Air Training Corps used the huts along the edge of the car park and beyond these can be seen the Riverside Café run by Mary Lax. Blagdon's Leather Works looms darkly in the background, with Hanratty's scrapyard off to the right. The road visible to the left of the Leather Works is Millburngate. In the modern photograph, the second phase of the Millburngate Centre dominates the scene. Imaginative use of pitched roofs and different levels have broken up what would otherwise have been a harsh roofline. The impression of smaller buildings that this creates is reminiscent of the town houses that were characteristic of Durham in years gone by.

*D*urham Castle dominates the foreground in a scene photographed from the cathedral tower. The left-hand side of original picture, taken in May 1970, gives some idea of the dramatic changes brought about by the construction of Millburngate House and the roads that pushed through the area in the 1960s. Millburngate House, left of centre, occupies the site of the old Durham City Gas Works and a terrace of houses, Castle View. One remaining gasholder was still in use at the time and can be seen behind the blocks of offices. Towards the top left, the widened A691 takes a new route from the railway bridge down to the Millburngate roundabout – the vehicles to the left of the new road are standing on the original thoroughfare. For years after the old picture was taken, the cleared areas around Millburngate House were used as car parks. The modern picture shows how these open spaces have disappeared beneath the Millburngate Centre and the new town houses of Highgate.

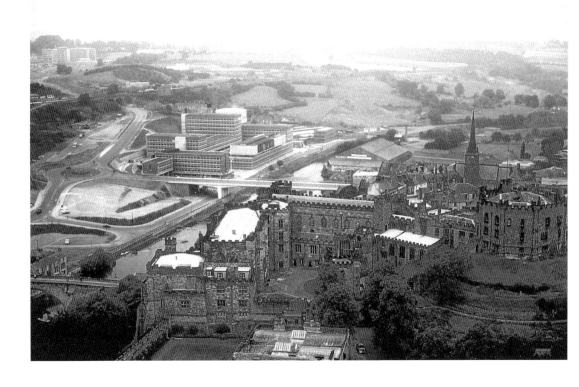

The construction of the Millburngate Shopping Centre was an essential aspect of the city's redevelopment plans. To make way for it, some older properties, like the four terraced houses shown in the old photograph, had to be removed. The old scene, captured in the early 1970s shows the uninhabited buildings shortly before demolition. The modern view has a skyline that is surprisingly unchanged. Although a furniture store and apartments have replaced the terrace, the buildings on the left of the old picture have been retained and enhanced. The building that housed the Five Ways Inn still stands. It was a pizzeria in recent times but is currently unoccupied, awaiting a new business. To the right of the former inn is the gable end of a tiny cottage, which dates from the fourteenth century and is now occupied by Plant Art Florists.

This old photograph of Millburngate was taken before the First World War by William Arthur Bramwell. A jeweller by trade, Bramwell was also a keen amateur photographer who captured many scenes in the city around the turn of the twentieth century. He was a founder member of the Durham City Camera Club, which was established in 1892. Although the club was disbanded after a decade, it re-emerged for a while after 1911 and finally assumed its present incarnation as Durham Photographic Society in 1947. The scene which attracted Bramwell's eye shows the cobbled street leading down to a short offshoot called the Horse Hole. This lane, off to the left of the two men in the road, led down to the river. Behind the men, Millburngate curves around

towards North Road. The Barley Sheaf Inn can be seen behind the street lamp and, immediately to the right of the pub, are two very old cottages. The cottages dated from the sixteenth century and were at the centre of a conservation row when the area was scheduled for clearance in the 1930s. It was decided that their condition had deteriorated too much to warrant saving and they were demolished, along with all the other houses seen here. The modern picture shows traffic waiting at the new Millburngate roundabout, with the shopping centre on the left taking the place of the old buildings.

3

Silver Street and the Market Place

Busy traffic at the south-western corner of the
Market Place in the 1960s.

A view from Framwellgate Bridge, showing the lower end of Silver Street, *c.* 1950. The origin of Silver Street's name is uncertain, but it is possible that a mint belonging to the Prince Bishops was once situated here. This end of the bridge was also the site of one of the old city gates, Smithgate.

The old picture shows the boarded-up frontage of the Cash Boot Company, closed after occupying this spot for many years. The Castle Hotel can be seen on the extreme right, with A.E. Pierce, optician, next door at No. 17. The traffic lights seen next to the figure were part of a system to control the flow of vehicles to and from the Market Place – Silver Street was too narrow to accommodate two-way traffic. The modern picture shows that the structure of this part of the street has remained largely unchanged, although a two-storey building has replaced the Cash Boot premises. Pedestrianisation has enabled the tarmac to be replaced by more attractive setts and flagstones.

*T*he narrowness of Silver Street is evidence of its medieval origins and is clearly shown in this early 1930s scene. The bus in the distance practically fills the road as vehicles move up the hill, having just been signalled through by the traffic lights lower down. The two boys hurrying along with their handcart are no doubt hoping to make it before they meet traffic

coming down the other way. The shops that crowd in on both sides show the same variety as would be seen on any high street, then or now. Bailes', printers and stationers, can be seen on the extreme left, followed by the shoe display of Freeman Hardy and Willis, with the cleaners, Pullar's of Perth, further up. To the right, Ramsbottom's butchers is sandwiched between two dairy product outlets – the canopied Meadow Dairy and the Maypole Dairy, sporting the globe-shaped lights. In the new picture, those in need of retail therapy enjoy the much safer and cleaner environment the modern street affords.

When George Greenwell started his grocery business in the 1860s, he could hardly have imagined it would still be trading at the same place over a hundred years later. After having had a shop near the Market Place for a few years, Greenwell moved to Albert House, 33 Silver Street, which was formerly a pub. He enlarged the premises by taking over No. 32 next door, above which the Dunelm Café was later established. The old photograph shows four of the smartly uniformed waitresses posing outside the entrance. Over the years, the grocer's shop gained a reputation for its good service and variety of produce and it became something of an institution in the city. Greenwell's closed in the early 1980s, much to the dismay of its many loyal customers. The modern

picture shows that a clothing shop has taken over the ground floor, while a beauty salon occupies the rooms of the former café, with the distinctive first-floor window still recognisable. The original shop next door has been replaced by the city's main post office. Removal of the façade of No. 32 has revealed that the building has a very old timber-framed structure, a feature that has been discovered elsewhere in Silver Street during renovations.

*T*he Rose and Crown Hotel stood where the Market Place meets Silver Street. It had a long history and it is said that King Charles II was once received there. In the latter part of the seventeenth century it was owned by Sir John Duck, a wealthy citizen who, according to legend, was set on the road to riches when a raven dropped a gold coin at his feet. Duck's grand house was just across the street from the Rose and Crown. The photograph of 1923 shows that the hotel not only had 'good stabling' at the centre door but also had its own motor garage. On the right of the picture is Battensby's drapers, who had occupied Nos 1 and 2 Silver Street for many years. In the late 1920s the Rose and Crown was demolished to make way for the Woolworths store that stands there today. Albion House, Battensby's old premises, was taken down in 1937 to be replaced with a branch of Marks and Spencer.

*C*onsidering the inherently static nature of most statues, the figure of Neptune in Durham's Market Place has had a remarkable life as a traveller. Presented to the city in 1729 by George Bowes MP, the statue was symbolic of an unfulfilled plan to link Durham to the Tyne by canal. The old picture, taken around 1860, shows the God of the Sea perched on a pant which was the source of fresh water for the Market Place. This old pant was demolished a short time later and Neptune was reinstalled above a fountain for the following forty years. In 1902 he took residence over a new pant, but by

1926 he was becoming too much of an obstacle to motor traffic and it was decided to relocate him to Wharton Park in the north of the city. The toll of time, vandalism and eventually a lightning strike in 1979 put an end to the statue's trip to the park. Neptune was to rise again, however, after another excursion – this time to Shropshire for restoration. In 1991 he returned to the Market Place, as the new picture shows, standing proudly, but without the support of his anchor.

*T*his 1920s picture of the Market Place recalls a time when the days of horse-drawn transport were coming to an end. The milkman's horse and cart, complete with milk churns, look rather out of place beside the mass of cars and motorcycles that dominate the scene. The cart is standing outside an arched doorway which was the entrance to Lloyds Bank and to the right of this is Hepworth's clothiers, who had recently moved here from their premises in Saddler Street. Donkin's tobacconist is at No. 22, then Pullar's of Perth, a cleaning and dyeing firm. The Prudential Assurance Company can be seen behind the men standing next to the cars. Today's picture shows the new occupants of the largely unchanged buildings and how traffic restrictions have made parking in the Market Place a rarity.

*T*he Coronation of King George V, on 19 June 1911, was marked by huge celebrations all over the country. Durham was no exception, as this photograph of the Market Place shows. Neptune's pant is covered with evergreens and decorated with the Royal Coat of Arms. To the left of the pant is one of the Venetian masts which circled the Market Place. Red, white and blue streamers stretched between these masts to give the impression of maypoles and each was surmounted by a Union flag. Electric arc lamps were used to illuminate the scene at night, one of which can be seen on the right. The modern picture shows the new Boots building to the left and how Neptune has been repositioned, but otherwise it's just an ordinary day. One wonders when, or if, it could all happen again.

Durham's market has a history that goes back to the early twelfth century. Since then, countless numbers of stallholders have set out their wares in the Market Place, hoping to persuade the public to part with their money. This 1930s picture shows such a stallholder, busying himself with the rabbits he is preparing for sale. Behind the stall, the traffic makes its way around the Londonderry statue, with the assistance of a policeman installed in the white-domed police box, just right of centre. Left of the police box, the white sign on the railings indicates the entrance to the gentlemen's lavatories, located beneath ground level. By 1975, traffic had been reduced sufficiently to do away with the police box (by then a second version) and the toilets disappeared forever beneath the flagstones of the enlarged area for pedestrians only. Today, cars have been squeezed out to the eastern side of the Market Place, allowing shoppers to browse in a quieter and safer environment.

*D*urham's Indoor Market, situated beneath the Town Hall, was opened in 1852. It occupied a large building that had, over previous centuries, served as a guildhall, an inn, a factory, a workhouse and a school. The old photograph gives an elevated view of the market stalls at the opening of the Durham County Hospital bazaar in 1935. In the late

1990s the market was given a major facelift, including a new stone floor, a balcony bistro, Victorian-style lighting and lift access at the rear of the building. The revamped market was officially opened by the Prime Minister, Tony Blair, in December 1996. Today's picture shows a much improved shopping environment, with the new wooden stalls topped with bright, striped canopies.

Saddler Street to Palace Green

The upper section of Saddler Street
on a winter's day, *c.* 1960.

An atmospheric image from the very early years of photography shows the junction of Saddler Street and Elvet Bridge in about 1860. The tall building in the centre was home to Michael and George Bailes, boot and shoemakers. To the extreme left is Robert Young's provisions store and the birdcage hanging just to the right of this identifies the premises of William Marshall, cooper and basket-maker. The Bailes shop is of interest because it stood at 29 Saddler Street, an address that does not exist any more. Nos 27 to 31 were demolished in 1865, which meant that Bailes had to relocate his business to No. 32, remaining there until the late 1880s. Today, Bailes' second shop houses a clothing repair and alteration business, while a Chinese restaurant occupies the first floor.

Shopkeepers have always tried to lure customers into their establishments with attractive window displays and this is a stunning example from the early years of the twentieth century. William Oliver was a butcher who traded as a fish and game dealer at 70 Saddler Street. Before Oliver took it over in 1904, the shop had been Caldcleugh's printers and stationers. Oliver stayed until the late 1920s, but fish and game continued to be sold here for many years afterwards, with T. Harland occupying the premises after Oliver, followed by A. McDonald in the early 1950s. The Scorpio shoe shop now occupies No. 70, setting out its goods on the street in a manner reminiscent of the poultry display in the old photograph.

*I*n the distant past, the section of Saddler Street shown in the pictures was known as Fleshergate, 'the butchers' street'. The old photograph shows the street in about 1930, by which time the butchers seem to have disappeared, but other trades are in abundance. A walk along the street from the left would take you past Mason's chemists and Harland's fishmongers, with Olive Tripcony's handicraft shop on the first floor. T.F. Hiller's music shop was at No. 71, followed by Coyne's drapers and the House of Andrews bookshop.

Across the road, a lady is passing by Docherty's the Drapers and the corner of Walter Wilson's grocers can be seen on the extreme right. Today's slightly lower viewpoint takes in the top of the Magdelene Steps as well as the modern shops – none of the old ones remain. However, above and to the left of the distant car, the huge teapot, which marked the House of Andrews in the shop's later years, is still there.

*R*oadworks such as these, photographed at the top of Elvet Bridge around 1920, must have been a nightmare for the motorists of the day. The narrow road was part of the main north-south route through the city and any closure resulted in lengthy diversions, so it was essential that the maintenance was done quickly. Sometimes, when major work was necessary, gangs of workers would

toil through the night under powerful electric arc lights to get the job done. In the old picture, the group of men taking a breather are standing outside Kennedy's umbrella shop, while behind them, on the corner, Walter Wilson's is having a tea sale. The modern image shows how the road surface has changed yet again – now designed with pedestrians in mind. The Magdelene Steps, obscured by spoil in the old picture, are now visible on the left in a much improved state, embellished with railings and a sculpture.

This old photograph, taken around 1900, shows the south-eastern corner of Palace Green. The building on the left of the picture is the southern end of Bishop Cosin's Almshouses, which was also the site of Bishop Langley's School for Common Singing in the fifteenth century. In 1876 the University Museum moved here from the Old Fulling Mill by the river. Typically for a museum of that time, its exhibits were amazingly varied, ranging from ancient Roman artefacts to a Chinaman's pigtail! The museum was always too small to house its collection and by 1916 much of it had been dispersed to other parts of the university. Eventually the museum moved back to its original riverside home. The low stone building and the stables at the centre of the picture were demolished to prepare for the neo-Gothic Pemberton Building, opened in 1931 to provide additional lecture rooms for the university. The new photograph shows the building as it is today.

*T*hree splendid old cars are shown parked at Palace Green on a snowy day in February 1912. They stand in front of two buildings now in the possession of the university, but formerly the property of the Church. The building to the left was originally the County Court House. It was rebuilt as the Diocesan Registry in 1822, before the Durham Union Debating Society occupied it after 1935. The taller building to the right is of more recent origin, in the 1850s this was the entrance to a courtyard behind the Registry. Off to the right of this building is the Library of Bishop Cosin, which still houses his collection of books, some of which predate 1500. In 1978, the University Library moved in, expanding from the Registry building into the Cosin's Library. Today's photograph, while showing that little has changed on this side of Palace Green, does say something about the development of the motor car in the intervening years.

*D*urham Castle is the city's oldest building; dating from 1072 it predates the cathedral by some twenty years. It became the palace of the Prince Bishops of Durham, religious men who wielded great secular power in the region. As one of the England's best preserved Norman castles, it has attracted millions of visitors over the years. Three such visitors, the Edwardian family in the old picture, sit on the steps at the entrance to the Great Hall, one of the country's largest and most impressive of its type. The photograph shows how the exterior stonework of the hall, built in the thirteenth and fourteenth centuries by Bishops Bek and Hatfield, was showing

distinct signs of wear and tear. At the time, the castle itself was in dire need of structural restoration, but it was not until the 1930s that the major work was begun, including the strengthening of the outer walls to prevent them tumbling into the River Wear. The castle has been the home of University College since 1832 and the Great Hall is now used as a dining hall for the students. The three young rugby players seen in the modern picture stand in front of the rejuvenated entrance as they discuss the finer points of the game.

5

Elvet

A group of workers at McIntyre's carriage works at Elvet waterside, in the early 1900s. The firm later branched out into auto engineering in New Elvet.

As county town, Durham held Assizes, the principal courts of the county. This 1903 photograph shows the judges making their way from the castle to the courts in Elvet and doing it in fine style. In later years they would have to make do with a limousine, but at this time it was a horse-drawn coach, complete with footmen and a police guard of honour. The picture is of Elvet Bridge and was taken from what is now the Swan and Three Cygnets pub. The coach is just passing a farrier's forge, which was also used as a veterinary surgery, while further down the street are Brooke's fruiterer and florist and the Ship Inn. The buildings in the old picture still remain today and are occupied by an Italian restaurant.

*E*lvet Waterside as seen from the steps leading down from Elvet Bridge. Most of the buildings seen across the river have been demolished to make way for the main through road bridge of 1976, which is visible on the left of the new picture. Traffic formerly crossed over Elvet Bridge itself (just out of the photograph to the right) and passed through the Market Place. The building on the right with the round light in the gable remains today, and is presently the Swan and Three Cygnets pub. In former days it saw use as a carpet shop and an electrical retailer.

*M*uch of New Elvet has changed beyond recognition in the last fifty years. The building of the university's Elvet Waterside complex was responsible for the demolition of a large proportion of the western side of the street. One such casualty was the building which once housed Fowler and Armstrong's garage, seen in the old picture. The firm moved to new premises across the street in the early 1950s, after which the old garage was run by Billy MacIntyre and Albert Mole, dealing in Hillman and Triumph cars. The new picture shows the roadway which now occupies the site of the garage, with residential flats, built in 2001, to the right of it.

*A*rchie Fowler and Mr Armstrong moved their business (previous photograph) in the early 1950s to this site, further up New Elvet. There they continued their Austin dealership in a brand new building with a larger forecourt. The old photograph of June 1952 shows a Morris 8 van and a motorbike parked on Court Lane and it is interesting to note that the main road of New Elvet, at the bottom of the picture, is still surfaced with setts. By this time the garage was selling Esso petrol rather than Shell, but still from hand-cranked pumps. In the early 1990s the site was redeveloped and is now the Orchard House complex of flats.

*O*n 10 May 1910 King George V, the present queen's grandfather, acceded to the throne on the death of his father, Edward VII. The event was proclaimed with full civic dignity at the neo-classical portico of Durham Assize Court, built adjoining the Durham Prison complex. A solemn crowd turned out for the event, which featured the Lord Lieutenant of the County and Durham's mayor and corporation. Today the Assize Court is Durham Crown Court. The façade of the building hasn't changed much in the intervening years and the courtrooms inside are still the stage for some of the North East's most serious criminal trials. Here a pair of young barristers make their way inside.

*A*t the turn of the nineteenth century, Durham Workmen's Club stood across the road from the Royal County Hotel, at 2 Old Elvet. In 1890 the building had been the Royal Mail Inn, but by 1898 it had become the Cycle Inn, which for a few years also took over No. 3. Durham Workmen's Club Ltd established itself in the street in 1902, but it was only to have a brief presence. By 1908 the club had been replaced by Stanton's Fruit and Fish Merchants, who occupied one of four new shops that had been installed on this section of the street. Stanton's is still selling fish in Durham, although not in Old Elvet. An estate agent and a florist now stand on the site of the Workmen's Club.

*B*enjamin Gleason stands in the doorway of his shop at 55 New Elvet, in this photograph taken about 1910. His grandfather and father had both been tinsmiths, the latter, Thomas Gleason, having moved to the New Elvet shop from Claypath in 1883. Benjamin

took over when his father died in the 1890s and ran it with the help of his uncle and later his son, Alexander. The business survived until the 1940s, when it was operating as Gleason's General Dealers. By that time Alexander had his own well-established shop on South Street. The modern picture shows the view today, with Dunelm House standing in place of the tinsmith's shop.

These three buildings once stood at the top end of New Elvet, just before the junction with Church Street. The shop on the right and the two houses next to it are all derelict and awaiting the bulldozer. Older Elvet residents still remember the houses and businesses which occupied this part of New Elvet and recall that they were in poor condition in the 1950s and '60s, just prior to demolition. The area had to be cleared to make way for Ove Arup's concrete Students' Union building, Dunelm House, which was completed in 1965 and which is shown in the new picture.

*T*his view of the cathedral was taken just south of Stockton Road and dates from about 1900. At that time, Elvet Colliery, seen at the left of the old picture, was in operation and producing coal for domestic and industrial use in the city. The pit, which was sunk in the 1820s, employed between fifty and a hundred miners at any one time, but the number of underground workers decreased steadily as the years went by. Eventually, flooding problems led to the pit being abandoned in 1908. In 1924 the university established its science site here with the opening of the brick and stone Dawson Building. The new picture shows how the laboratories have spread across the area – this despite contractors having to deal with six shafts from the old mine while the new buildings went up.

6

The Gala

Thousands of miners and their families wait for
the speech-making at 'The Big Meeting', *c.* 1930.

*D*urham Miners' Gala is the longest-established and largest event of its kind in the country. 'The Big Meeting', as it is known locally, can be traced back to mass meetings held in the 1830s. Before the railway closures of the 1960s, whole parties would arrive by train at Durham Station. Led by the colliery band and lodge officials, miners and their families would follow their banner in procession through the streets. The photographs portray two bands, separated in time by fifty years, in North Road as they begin their journey to the university playing fields at the racecourse. The march would continue by way of Framwellgate Bridge, the Market Place, Elvet Bridge and past the County Hotel, where high-ranking politicians would look down at the throng from the famous balcony. Nowadays, the local rail services have disappeared and participants are more likely to arrive by motor coach. Their route remains the same but the 'big name' politicians are not so often seen.

*T*his 1936 picture shows the Sacriston Lodge banner being paraded up Silver Street. Benny Lambert, Lodge Secretary, is second from left. Third from left is ex-MP and miners' agent, Jack Swan. Fourth from left is Jack Lawson, who was later to become a lord. Under the banner on the left with a cigarette is Fred Lawson and right is Tom Johnson. The new picture depicts mining veterans who were called into mining service during the Second World War as 'Bevin Boys'. They were named after the then Minister of Labour and National Service, Ernest Bevin, who directed that 50,000 additional men should be recruited to help meet coal production demands for the war effort. From December 1943 to the end of the war a total of 49,859 young men of call-up age were selected by ballot systems to work in the pits. Following four weeks' training they would work underground, often in tough conditions, for an average wage of £3 10s. Now they carry their banner with justifiable pride.

*B*oth photographs here show a mass of people enjoying a day out at 'The Big Meeting'. The images are seventy years apart and superficially there are obvious differences. Not so obvious is the effect that time has had on communities. At the time of the earlier picture, mines were still in private ownership and life was hard for a miner and his family. At the time of nationalisation in 1947, the 145 coal mines in the county achieved high output and the future

looked bright. However, the second half of the twentieth century saw pit closures gradually reducing the numbers employed underground. The process accelerated during the 1980s and by 1993 all of County Durham's mines had closed. In 1994, the industry returned to private ownership. Throughout this period, there was a corresponding reduction in banner numbers at the Gala. It seemed that the great annual event had had its day. In the late 1990s however, a revival took place and in recent years attendances have shown an encouraging increase.

*A*ll the bands, the banners and their followers eventually arrive at the racecourse. The instruments are carefully laid down and the banners erected while all gather around the platform to hear what is to be said about important matters of work and employment. Political speeches have always been at the hub of the day's proceedings. The crowd in the photograph from 1935 are listening intently to a speaker – an MP perhaps, whose words would be focused on the political issues of the day, or a union leader, calling for better conditions in the mines. Now the mines lie redundant. At a present-day Gala the guest speakers may cover broader issues, but their words will still be meaningful. The crowd will express their agreement, or disagreement, just as they always did. Still will be heard the call for workers' rights, still can be seen the familiar gestures emphasising and 'driving home' the speaker's key words. The spirit of Durham Miners' Gala goes on.

After the speeches on the racecourse, three lodge bands and banners together with their many followers make their way to the cathedral for a special service. These are selected in advance and each year different bands take part – it is always considered an honour. The Dean of Durham normally conducts the service and music by the brass bands is a major part of the proceedings. Whatever one's religious background, Durham Miners' Cathedral Service is a memorable experience. It is a time to remember the many who have perished in the Durham mines. The banners are held high and carried with

great pride; the music is played with much feeling and generates great emotion in the hearts of the congregation. The early photograph here is of Washington 'F' Pit Lodge Banner leaving the cathedral after the service, *c.* 1950. The later image is of Lambton Lodge Banner. The much smaller gathering of onlookers suggests a decline in public interest, yet in 2005 attendance was estimated to be 50,000 – the highest for forty years.

Claypath

Claypath in the early 1960s. The buildings to the left of the picture were demolished when the Claypath underpass was constructed.

The lower part of Claypath lost shops and other buildings when an underpass was constructed there in 1966. This early 1970s picture clearly shows the large gap that this opened up between the Market Place and Claypath. The physical separation was of particular concern to traders, who feared the street might become a backwater. Today's picture shows that, despite the inevitable gap, Claypath has been regenerated by the creation of Millennium Square, with its Gala Theatre and new City Library. The complex replaced the gas showrooms and the car park seen at the centre of the old photograph. At the left of the new picture is the business end of the city's road toll system – the first of its kind in the country. Motorists passing through the Market Place, perhaps travelling to the cathedral, pay a fee at this point on their return. The scheme has cut traffic using this route by 85 per cent, while at the same time pedestrian activity has increased.

*J*ames Fowler opened his grocery shop at No. 99 Claypath in the 1840s. Early in his tenancy he gained a lot of goodwill in the city for the way he 'helped out' miners during a prolonged strike action. This act evoked a lot of customer loyalty and perhaps contributed to the success of the business, which was to remain at this point in the street until the 1966 Claypath underpass arrived. Fowler's was, for a time,

custodian of the famous teapot, which now resides in Saddler Street. Traditionally the sign of a grocer, the giant teapot started life above a shop in the Market Place and then moved to Gilesgate post office, before arriving at Fowler's. The modern picture shows the underpass (to the left) and slip road where the shop once stood.

*I*t is somewhat surprising to find in the heart of the Durham mining community, with its proud tradition of support for the Labour Party and the Trade Union movement, such overt support for an extreme right-wing organisation such as the British Union of Fascists. The first picture dating from about 1936 shows their office in what was then one of Durham's busiest streets, only a few steps away from the Market Place. The poster on the left says, 'Fascists Intervene in Durham Pit Dispute.' This is an indication of the conflict between the Fascists and the National Union of Mineworkers. The Fascists blamed the Union for the distress and unemployment which the North East experienced in the years between the wars. The second picture could be seen as a demonstration of the international community we have become today.

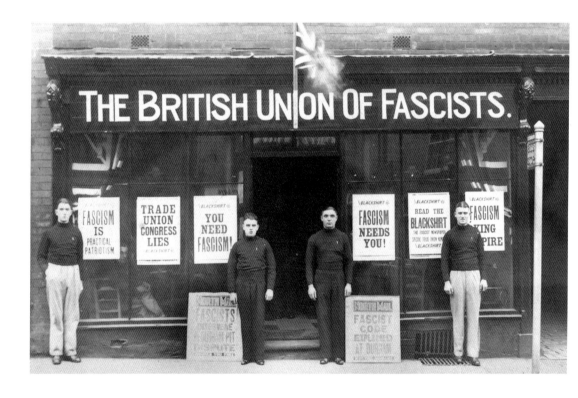

*P*rovidence Row leads from Claypath down to Freeman's Place and The Sands area. The street has changed its name more than once since the sixteenth century, originally being called Woodman's Chair, meaning Woodman's Lane, before taking on its present name in the nineteenth century. The old picture harks back to the days when horses were the main form of motive power and shows the hayloft of the Corporation Stables, which occupied Nos 5 and 6 Providence Row before the Second World War. The chimney at the left of the picture shows the position of the Provincial Laundries, which were later replaced by a Post Office sorting office.

*D*urham City Branch of Durham County Library first opened in 1930. At that time, the city provided the premises and the county funded the library, which was initially housed in the Burlison Art Gallery. In 1933 the City Council made a decision to purchase the old Police Building on Claypath, but not necessarily for a library. The library was soon installed there, however, and the early picture shows the building, with its identifying torch

symbol above street level. A Miss F.E. Cook of Sunderland was appointed librarian and she had the help of one assistant and a caretaker. The library remained in Claypath until 1961 when it moved to newly built premises on South Street. The old premises have recently been extensively renovated and now function as an Indian restaurant – but the torch still remains.

*T*he College of St Hild and St Bede is the largest college in Durham University, occupying 16 acres of tree-lined grounds near the banks of the River Wear. Back in 1910 the principal of St Hild's College was Miss Winifred Hindmarsh (right), who, in those days, went by the title of governor. The highly respected Miss Hindmarsh retired in the 1920s and in her honour students created a nature pond in the college grounds. It still exists today amid the college gardens, complete with

wildlife including newts. The College of the Venerable Bede was founded in 1839. It was a Church of England education college for the training of male teachers. As St Bede's and St Hild's were concerned principally with educational training, they were not fully integrated with the university. They existed separately and independently for many years but in 1975 they amalgamated and assumed a title that combined both names. Today the college still specialises in the training of schoolteachers. The current principal of St Hild and St Bede College is Dr Alan Pearson BSc PhD who is seen here in his office. Dr Pearson is proud of his college's many fine facilities which include, among the excellent sporting and academic facilities, a chapel, a theatre and a cinema.

The Lecture Room at St Hild's College, Durham, pictured in about 1910. The college was founded in 1857 by the Church of England to train schoolmistresses and has been part of Durham University since its merger with St Bede's in 1975. The college has some of the university's best sporting and academic facilities and has its own tennis, squash and netball courts. Today's picture of the same lecture room, taken some ninety years later, reflects the changes in education technology. It is now the college's computer room, the largest computer room in all of Durham's colleges. Note how the dress of today's students is much less formal.

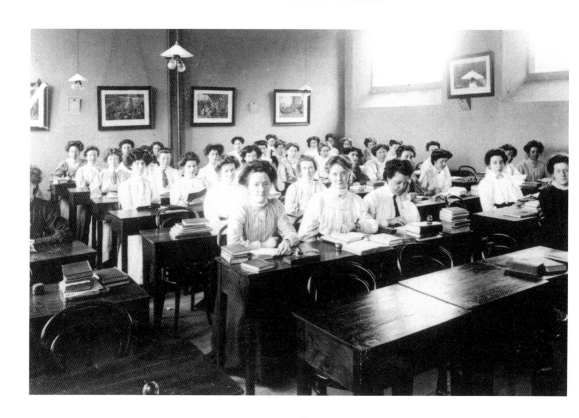

*T*he Palladium cinema opened in 1929 amidst considerable controversy. It was the first cinema in the city to be granted a seven-day licence and the fact that it would be operating on a Sunday drew criticism from such groups as the Lord's Day Observance Society. The cinema's licence was granted on the understanding that Sunday opening would be restricted to a couple of hours in the evening and the programme for that day was approved by the police. The first film shown was *The Garden of Allah*, but

when the photograph here was taken, the main feature was *Love Letters*, which dates the image to about 1945. Like many small cinemas across the country, the Palladium saw declining audiences as the years passed and it closed in 1976. After a period of time as a bingo hall, the cinema building fell into disuse, although the original interior is largely intact and some of the seating is still in place. Today's photograph shows the old picture house with its display panels still fastened to the walls outside. The Maltman Hotel, seen between the cinema and the church in the early picture, has gone altogether, with its place being taken by an 'alternative clothing and jewellery shop'.

Gilesgate Station was the first of several railway stations to have served Durham over the past 150 years. Opened in 1844 as part of the Newcastle & Darlington Junction Railway, the station was the terminus of a branch line coming in from Belmont on the city's eastern outskirts. The line carried passengers and freight until 1857, when the present main line station opened. Following this, passengers used the new station and Gilesgate became goods only. The old photograph shows the station shortly before it closed and the track was removed in the mid-1960s. The A690 link road from the A1 later followed the line of the track into the city, passing behind the old station building just before reaching the Gilesgate roundabout. J. & G. Archibald's store moved into the old station for a while, before the building was redeveloped as the Travelodge Hotel, seen in the modern photograph.

8

Along the River

A riverside view from the old gasworks, taken
before the building of the ice rink in 1940.

*C*rook Hall, one of the oldest inhabited houses in the city, was built around AD 1300. Some of the original building, including the hall with its gallery, still stands today. The single light trefoil-headed windows are very well preserved. In 1346 John de Coupland spent the night in Crook Hall prior to the battle of Neville's Cross. The next day he was the victorious captor of the Scottish king. Later he was to reside in the hall from 1360 to 1372. These views show the rear of the Georgian wing and illustrate how the present owners have converted the old clothes drying facility to a sitting area for serving teas. Crook Hall and its gardens are open to the public on Sunday afternoons in the summer, and every day during August.

After the building of the cathedral a number of religious institutions grew up around Durham dedicated to the care of the sick and the elderly. Some also provided hospitality for pilgrims and travellers. One such was situated on the banks of the river next to a fish trap, hence the name Kepier. It was founded by Bishop Le Puiset about 1180. These views show the inside of the gatehouse, which was probably rebuilt in the fourteenth century following damage by a Scottish raiding party. The buildings adjoining the gatehouse were originally a stone base with a half-timbered first floor. The early picture would seem to indicate that this was replaced by brickwork at some stage. This must then have been removed as the later picture shows a much lower roofline.

A happy group of skaters pose for the camera at Durham City Ice Rink in October 1947, just seven years after its opening. It was the brainchild of John Smith, who owned an ice-making works just across the river. At first, the ice rink was covered by a huge canopy but, after this was destroyed in a gale, a new building with a permanent roof was completed in 1945. Smith was keen to develop the competitive side of the sport and established the Durham Wasps ice hockey team just after the Second World War. The Wasps went on to be the premier team in Britain during the 1980s, when they won many national titles, but Durham lost its ice hockey stars in 1995 when Sir John Hall bought the team for his Newcastle United Sporting Club. The ice rink closed in 1996 and the Kascada bowling alley, shown in the new picture, has taken its place, providing the city with a new leisure activity.

*T*he idea of a bridge linking Framwellgate to Claypath on the other side of the River Wear was first mooted in the 1870s. It was nearly a century before this came to fruition in the form of Millburngate Bridge, seen being constructed in the old photograph. The project was part of the first phase of road and bridge building which was planned to divert 15,000 vehicles a day from the city centre. Construction began in May 1964 and the contractors, Holst Ltd, poured 10,000 cubic metres of concrete into the structure before its completion in April 1967. Millburngate House, which was being built at the same time, had not then reached sufficient height to make it visible in the old picture, but it can be seen at the left end of the bridge in the new image. Millburngate Centre is also prominent today on the left bank of the river.

*P*aradise Lane was
a narrow, winding
passage that ran from the
lower end of Claypath,
opposite St Nicholas' church,
down to the river at Elvet
Bridge. The name Paradise
was hardly appropriate
however, for it had long
been one of the poorer
quarters of the city and was notorious for the
lamentable state of its housing and sanitation.
Along its eastern side was an open space called
Paradise Gardens, a large portion of which
was bought by Gilbert Henderson, the carpet
factory owner, in the 1830s. At that time, even
the Paradise Gardens were no Eden and one
nineteenth-century writer described a huge
dung heap which seemed to be a permanent
feature there. By the twentieth century there
was growing discontent with the state of

many of Durham's 'back streets', including
Paradise Lane. In May 1947, the *Durham
County Advertiser* commented, 'Durham can
never justify the claim that is made of it as
the most beautiful city in the land until some
attention has been paid to these "horrors" and
the place has been made presentable'. The old
photograph shown here was taken later that
same month. Today's picture shows the new
scene, with Paradise Lane and Gardens buried
beneath the Prince Bishop Shopping Centre.

*T*he beginning and the end of Durham City Branch Library and Central Reference Library are seen in these two pictures. Opened in November 1961, it promised more space, more books and 'probably the finest view of any library in the country', with its outlook over the river to the cathedral. The library was split into two levels, with the lending section at street level and the reference section below. It quickly became a success, with 115,000 books being issued per year, but as time passed it became apparent that it was not totally fulfilling

the city's needs. As the century came to an end, libraries wanted to expand the services they offered the public, and the relatively small South Street branch, with its poor access for the disabled, needed to be replaced by something better. When the concept of a new library at Claypath became a reality, the old one became redundant and was closed in 2002. The new image shows the site shortly after demolition in 2005.

 T his late nineteenth-
   century view
gives us a rare glimpse
of the original Baths Bridge. The wooden
footbridge, built in 1865 and paid for by public
subscription, was a convenient link between
Gilesgate, to the north of the river and Elvet,
to the south. It took its name from the Public
Baths and Wash Houses at its Southern end,
access to which had been a major factor in
its construction. In 1898, it was replaced by a
more robust (but uglier) metal structure which
was in use for sixty years before the present
Baths Bridge was built on the same site in
1962. The modern view shows a bridge which,
although made of concrete rather than wood,
has a strikingly similar design to the original.

*B*rown's Boathouse, close to Elvet Bridge, was a prominent landmark along the river for over a hundred years. In 1884, Joseph Brown obtained the boatbuilding firm from the Colpitts family, who sold out to concentrate on their main business as hoteliers. When Joseph died in 1947, his son Erik took over the reins. The firm became well known for producing wooden racing boats, both fours and eights, and the old picture, from 1956, shows such a craft outside the boathouse. Brown's also hired out rowing boats, canoes and punts to those wishing to 'mess about

on the river'. In the mid-1970s the boatbuilding tradition was continued when Clive Hole took over, forming Brown's Boathouse Ltd and, later, Durham River Trips utilising the *Prince Bishop* river cruiser. By 2000, however, developers had planning permission to demolish the boathouse and build a large, glass-fronted pub. This project had to be downsized because of engineering difficulties and the building itself was preserved as the Chase Boathouse Café Bar seen in today's picture.

*T*his view across the river towards Brown's Boathouse was taken shortly before the building of Durham's first multi-storey car park in 1975. The ruined remnants of Paradise Lane, soon to be swallowed up by the car park, are visible behind the wall on the left. In the distance, there is a rare glimpse of the rear of buildings on this side of the Market Place. The £1 million car park was relatively short-lived. It won an award for the design of its exterior walls, but its tight turns and unreliable ticket machines made it unpopular with many motorists. It was demolished to make way for the Prince Bishop Shopping Centre, opened in 1998 and shown in the new picture, which houses fifty shops and has its own parking facility for 400 cars.

*E*lvet Bridge has provided a vital link between the peninsula and the district of Elvet for centuries. First built in 1160, the bridge has been modified many times during its lifetime, including major reconstruction after the central arches were swept away in the Great Flood of 1771 and the doubling of its width in 1805. Two chapels (one at either end), medieval shops and a City Gate have all occupied the bridge in the past, but they had been long gone when the old photograph shown here was taken. Beyond the bridge in the old picture are the backs of buildings in Saddler Street and the Bailey. Brown's Boathouse can be seen to the right. The same viewpoint today shows the *Prince Bishop* river cruiser across the river from the new Chase Boathouse Café Bar.

9

Around the City

Harvesting at Potter's Bank, on the city's
south-eastern outskirts, in the early
twentieth century.

*S*herburn Road Estate, beyond Gilesgate on the edge of Durham, was built by the City Council in the 1930s to house families displaced by slum clearance schemes in the ancient city centre. Here on 13 and 14 May 1935, the residents helped George V celebrate his Silver Jubilee by staging a street party at the then newly built council estate. By the 1990s Sherburn Road Estate had become badly run down and the Council, in partnership with housing associations, embarked on a multi-million pound revitalisation scheme. Today most of the 1930s council houses have been completely modernised. Some have been demolished to make way for new executive homes while many streets have been bollarded to discourage through traffic, making the area safer for children and old people. Pylon-mounted CCTV cameras add to the sense of security.

*T*his was the scene in the canteen for visitors at Dryburn Hospital back in May 1951. For many years hardworking lady volunteers of the WRVS devoted their spare time to providing much-needed tea, coffee and light refreshments in this makeshift tearoom. Back in the 1950s the majority of visitors would have travelled to the hospital by bus and would have been much in need of a reviving cuppa. In those days hot meals would have been a rarity. Today the commercially managed Bede Restaurant offers a much wider range of drinks and food compared to the limited fayre that was on offer many years ago. Visitors and staff now enjoy first-class meals and light refreshments in the smart Bede Restaurant where panoramic windows give wide views across the city to the cathedral and the surrounding County Durham countryside.

George Hauxwell was a Yorkshireman born and bred and was an iron founder and engine builder by trade. He and his family moved to Durham in the 1860s where he set up a foundry and engineering works at Atherton Street, in the shadow of the railway viaduct. By the 1880s the works employed twenty-two men and eight boys. The firm specialised in making and erecting waterwheels and the works housed a huge lathe for their manufacture. To the left of centre in the old picture, the incongruous sight of a crane protruding from the terrace identifies the foundry. The business remained a family concern until well into the twentieth century. In 1971, a new road pushed through from the North Road roundabout and much of Atherton Street, including Hauxwell's, came down as a result. The construction of the road has had the not inconsiderable side-effect of showing off the viaduct to greater advantage, something that can be appreciated from the new picture.

*T*his picture, from the early 1960s, shows Williamson's butcher's shop at the bottom of Crossgate Peth. The shop, along with Clover Cottage, was situated by the roadside, a little in front of the terrace of houses that still makes up the street. Norman Williamson was a master butcher who was also involved in local politics. In 1961 he became Mayor of Durham and in his inaugural address he spoke of his conviction that Durham would always be a lovely city, despite the vast changes that would result from the proposed building of roads and bridges. At the time, he already knew that he was likely to be affected himself. Five years later the butcher's shop and Clover Cottage were demolished as part of the road improvement scheme. The old buildings in the centre of the old picture had a similar fate. The modern photograph shows a new traffic light system at this busy junction and, just beyond the lights, the appearance of new homes at St Margaret's Court.

In this 1920s shot a man, wearing the almost obligatory headgear of the cloth cap, makes his way up Crossgate, one of Durham's steepest streets. From this viewpoint, two spires, those of St Nicholas in the Market Place and the United Reform Church in Claypath, can be seen in the distance. On the extreme right of the picture, a small sign hangs above the doorway of J. Wise, Fruiterer. Wise came to Crossgate in 1898 and ran the shop until shortly before the Second World War. Further down the street, on the corner, a lamp on the wall identifies Ye Olde Elm Tree Inn. In the modern picture, the Elm Tree is still going strong, but some of the buildings above it, including the fruiterer's shop, were replaced by the Grape Lane Flats, built in the 1960s.

*T*his engraving, first published in the *London Illustrated News*, shows a cricket match at Durham's Racecourse, *c.* 1847. There had been racing on this large, open area by the river since the mid-1600s and, by the nineteenth century, Durham City Cricket Club was holding its fixtures there. In the late 1880s, the university took over the lease of the land and the racecourse was used as the university playing fields, as it still is today. Of interest, at the bottom right of the old picture, is the footbridge, now long gone, that crossed the river to the north bank. Today's image shows the view across the river to the sports ground – which naturally includes a cricket pitch.

The carpet manufacturing business was Durham's biggest employer for many years and was based at Freeman's Place, just downstream from the present Millburngate Bridge. Gilbert Henderson started his carpet factory here in 1815 and the Henderson family ran the firm until 1903, when they sold it to a company who turned out to be asset-strippers. The manager of Henderson's at the time, Hugh Mackay, found himself out of work, so he decided to set up in business himself, renting some of the Freeman's Place buildings to do so. The enterprise flourished and when Hugh Mackay died in 1924, his son, Laurence, took over and enlarged the works. In 1969,

an arson attack badly damaged part of the factory and after this production of Wilton carpets was switched to the firm's Dragonville site in the east of the city. Axminster production stayed at Freeman's Place until 1981, when it too moved to Dragonville and the riverside factory was closed down. The old picture shows the works in the process of being demolished. Today, the area is the focus of projects which will provide new and improved facilities for the city. The Gala Theatre and library are already in place and, behind the white barriers at the site of the former carpet factory, contractors are preparing the ground for a 500-space multi-storey car park, thirty-five residential apartments and an hotel.

*M*ountjoy Farm stands on a hill to the south-east of Durham's peninsula. The old picture, taken at the farm in April 1938, shows the farmer using horses to harrow his field – a scene that within a few years would become a thing of the past. The view from the hill was, and still is, spectacular, with the tower of St Oswald's church visible in front of the cathedral, standing proudly on the horizon. Mountjoy has a legend attached to it. According to the story, this was the hill where monks, searching for a resting place for St Cuthbert's body, came across a milkmaid looking for her cow. The maid directed them to a place called Dun Holm (Durham) and the saint was laid to rest there – the rest, as they say, is history.

Other local titles published by Tempus

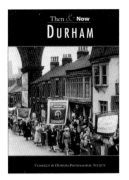

Durham Then and Now
DURHAM PHOTOGRAPHIC SOCIETY

Compiled by the Durham Photographic Society, *Durham Then & Now* is a fascinating collection of over 80 pairs of photographs that vividly illustrate the changing face of Durham. By contrasting views of the city and its people over the last century with modern scenes, we are granted a unique opportunity to witness the changes that have occurred in the city.

0 7524 1829 7

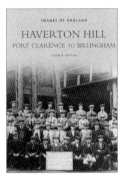

Haverton Hill Port Clarence to Billingham
COLIN H. HATTON

This nostalgic book of archive images with supporting captions tells the story of three rich and varied communities which made up an industrial area covering the north bank of the River Tees. It describes the rise and subsequent decline of the steel and chemical industries and the railways, as well as covering aspects of everyday life such as leisure, churches and chapels, schools, work and sport.

0 7524 3425 X

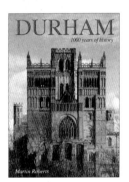

Durham 1000 Years of History
MARTIN ROBERTS

Durham is a World Heritage city of remarkable architectural richness, with the castle, cathedral and town forming three constant elements in a history spanning many centuries. The buildings of the years 1550-1860, as well as those of the modern city, are fully described, as are the city's magnificent riverbanks, parks and gardens in this fascinating book by Martin Roberts, himself an architect and member of the Institute of Historic Building Conservation.

0 7524 2537 4

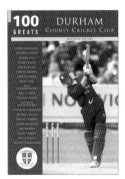

Durham County Cricket Club 100 Greats
MATTHEW APPLEBY

Durham, the youngest first-class county, has a record as proud as any other. During its 110 years as a Minor County it played 30 matches against international touring teams, as well as becoming the first Minor County side to beat a first-class side (Yorkshire) in 1973. With illustrations, biographies and statistics of Durham's finest cricketers, this book pays tribute to the men who are the county's cricketing history.

0 7524 3195 1

If you are interested in purchasing other books published by Tempus, or in case you have difficulty finding any Tempus books in your local bookshop, you can also place orders directly through our website

www.tempus-publishing.com